T0414222

At a Play

LEVEL 6

/a_e/
/ai/

DECODABLES

BY jump!

Teaching Tips

Orange Level 6

This book focuses on the phonemes **/a_e/ai/**.

Before Reading

- Discuss the title. Ask readers what they think the book will be about. Have them briefly explain why.
- Ask readers to say the name of each object on page 3. Which ones end in a_e? What letters and sounds do the names of the other objects end in?

Read the Book

- Encourage readers to break down unfamiliar words into units of sound. Then, ask them to string the sounds together to create the words.
- Urge readers to point out when the focused phonics phonemes appear in the text.

After Reading

- Encourage children to reread the book independently or with a friend.
- Ask readers to name other words with /a_e/ or /ai/ phonemes. On a separate sheet of paper, have them write the words out.

© 2024 Booklife Publishing
This edition is published by arrangement with Booklife Publishing.

North American adaptations © 2024 Jump!
5357 Penn Avenue South
Minneapolis, MN 55419
www.jumplibrary.com

Decodables by Jump! are published by Jump! Library.
All rights reserved. No part of this book may be reproduced in any form without written permission from the publisher.

Library of Congress Cataloging-in-Publication Data is available at www.loc.gov or upon request from the publisher.

ISBN: 979-8-88996-852-8 (hardcover)
ISBN: 979-8-88996-853-5 (paperback)
ISBN: 979-8-88996-854-2 (ebook)

Photo Credits
Images are courtesy of Shutterstock.com. With thanks to Getty Images, Thinkstock Photo and iStockphoto. Cover – Mikhail Tchkheidze. 2–3 – Alex Stemmers, Eky Studio, M. Unal Ozmen, Valentina Razumova, tobibambola, Creatus, Andrey_Kuzmin, VladyslaV Travel photo. 4–5 – Igor Bulgarin, Kozlik, 6–7 – T photography, A_Lesik. 8–9 – Jonas Petrovas. 10–11 – BG Plus2, Nacha Petchdawong. 12–13 – Yuriy Golub, Igor Bulgarin. 14–15 – Robert Kneschke, Kozlik. 16 – Shutterstock.

Which of these objects have a_e in their name?

Have you ever seen a play? Plays are not the same as movies. The performers are right there!

The performers may sing songs or just speak. Some plays have lots of props, costumes, and makeup. There are all sorts of different plays.

After you have paid, an usher may help you
to your seat.

Some theaters have seats on different levels.
You can look down on the play from up high.

When the play is about to start, it will go dark. Then, the drapes are pulled back and the play will start.

Drapes

An act is a part of the play. Some plays have three acts that make up the start, middle, and end.

The performers may be far away from the crowd. They paint lots of makeup on so the people in the back can see it.

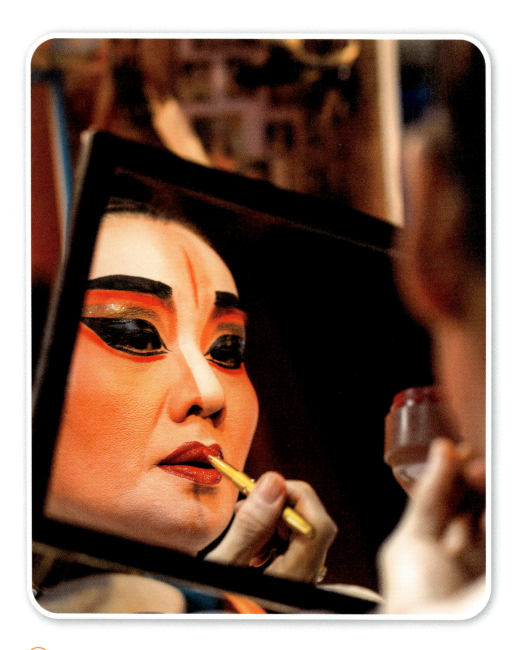

They may need new outfits or makeup as the play is still happening.

The performers have to speak up so the whole crowd can hear them. If they do not, people may just hear a faint sound.

In some plays, performers do not need to speak to tell a tale. They may just use their hands and not say a thing.

At the end, the performers bow as the crowd claps. They wave and wait for the clapping to finish.

You could make a play too. All you need to do is dress up and have fun!

Can you name the missing letters for each word?

tr___n

v__s__

pl__n__